RELIGIONS AROUND THE WORLD

Judaism

Katy Gerner

Marshall Cavendish
Benchmark

New York

This edition first published in 2009 in the United States of America by Marshall Cavendish Benchmark.

Marshall Cavendish Benchmark
99 White Plains Road
Tarrytown, NY 10591
www.marshallcavendish.us

First published in 2008 by
MACMILLAN EDUCATION AUSTRALIA PTY LTD
15–19 Claremont Street, South Yarra 3141

Visit our website at www.macmillan.com.au or go directly to www.macmillanlibrary.com.au

Associated companies and representatives throughout the world.

Library of Congress Cataloging-in-Publication Data

Gerner, Katy.
  Judaism / by Katy Gerner.
      p. cm. — (Religions around the world)
  Includes index.
  ISBN 978-0-7614-3170-1
  1. Judaism—Juvenile literature. I. Title.
  BM573.G47 2008
296—dc22
                              2008002850

Edited by Erin Richards
Text and cover design by Cristina Neri, Canary Graphic Design
Photo research by Legend Images
Illustration on p. 15 by Andy Craig and Nives Porcellato
Map courtesy of Geo Atlas; modified by Raul Diche

Printed in the United States

Acknowledgments

The author would like to thank Rabbi Chaim Rosenthal and Ellen Fiedler for their suggestions, their wisdom and their time spent reviewing this book.

The author and the publisher are grateful to the following for permission to reproduce copyright material:

Front cover photograph (main): Members of the high priesthood place their hands on a newborn baby to bless him, Israel © David Furst/AFP/Getty Images. Other cover images: Book background © Felix Möckel/iStockphoto; Ten Commandments © james steidl/iStockphoto; Menorah © Rafa Irusta/iStockphoto; Budapest Synagogue towers © Peter Spiro/iStockphoto; Wailing Wall, Jerusalem © Mark Weiss/iStockphoto; Star of David based on image by Georgios Kollidas/Shutterstock.

Photos courtesy of: AAP Image/AP Photo/Oded Balilty, **9**; AAP Image/AP Photo/Kathy Willens, **20** (bottom left); AAP Image/Comstock, **25** (top); © Nikolai Ignatiev/Alamy, **16**; © Israel images/Alamy, **29** (top); © Israelimages.com/Garo Nalbandian, **12** (bottom inset); © Ricki Rosen/CORBIS SABA, **23** (top); ANATOLIAN NEWS AGENCY/AFP/Getty Images, **7** (top); David Furst/AFP/Getty Images, **22**; Volker Hartmann/AFP/Getty Images, **28** (top); Photo by Anne Frank House, Amsterdam/Getty Images, **19** (bottom right); Guido Reni/The Bridgeman Art Library/Getty Images, **13** (top); Wojtek Laski/East News via Getty Images, **7** (bottom); Leland Bobbe/Stone/Getty Images, **21** (bottom); Photo by Carsten Koall/Getty Images, **15** (top); Mario Tama/Getty Images, **26**; Photodisc/Getty Images, **27** (right); © bratan007/iStockphoto, **32**; © Claudia Dewald/iStockphoto, **20** (right); © Rafa Irusta/iStockphoto, **3** (center), **31** (top); © Aman Khan/iStockphoto, **4** (bottom center left); © Vasko Miokovic/iStockphoto, **4** (center); © Owusu-Ansah/iStockphoto, **4** (bottom center right); © Richard Stamper/iStockphoto, **4** (bottom right); © james steidl/iStockphoto, **1** (center); © Bob Thomas/iStockphoto, **4** (bottom left); The Leo Baeck Institute, New York, **18** (bottom left); NASA Goddard Space Flight Center, **4** (center behind); © Caro/Alamy/Photolibrary, **6** (bottom); © Corky Buczyk/Shutterstock, **5** (bottom); © Boris Katsman/Shutterstock, **10**, **11** (top); © Leo/Shutterstock, **17** (top left); © Scott Rothstein/Shutterstock, **17** (bottom left); © Gordon Swanson/Shutterstock, **4** (top), **24**, **30** (top right); © Lisa F. Young/Shutterstock, **14** (right); Wikimedia Commons [The Yorck Project: 10.000 Meisterwerke der Malerei. DVD-ROM, 2002], **8** (left).

Photos used in book design: book background © Felix Möckel/iStockphoto, **14**; parchment background © Andrey Zyk/iStockphoto, **6**, **12**, **13**, **18**, **19**; scroll background © james steidl/iStockphoto, **8**; Star of David based on image by Georgios Kollidas/Shutterstock, **1**, **3**, **5**, **17**; Wailing Wall, Jerusalem © Mark Weiss/iStockphoto, **3**, **5**, **6**, **12–13**, **19**, **23**, **25**, **29**, **31**.

In memory of Grandma, Papa, Marny, Pop, Unc, and Mum

1 3 5 6 4 2

Contents

Glossary words

When a word is printed in **bold**, you can look up its meaning in the Glossary on page 31.

World Religions

Religion is a belief in a supernatural power that must be loved, worshipped, and obeyed. A world religion is a religion that is practiced throughout the world. The five core world religions are Christianity, Islam, Hinduism, Buddhism and Judaism.

People practicing a religion follow practices that they believe are pleasing to their god or gods. Followers read sacred **scriptures** and may worship either privately at home or in a place of worship. They often carry out special rituals, such as when a baby is born, a couple gets married, or someone dies. Religious people have beliefs about how they should behave in this life, and also about life after death.

Learning about world religions can help us to understand each other's differences. We learn about the different ways people try to lead good lives and make the world a better place.

World religions are practiced by many people of different cultures.

Judaism

Judaism is one of the oldest religions practiced today. It was begun by ancient Hebrews about 1300 BCE or even earlier. It is the oldest religion that worships one god only. Jews worship God and obey his laws, which are recorded in the Hebrew Bible. They practice special ceremonies and rites, which they believe God has chosen especially for them. They worship both in **synagogues** and at home.

The Star of David is the universal symbol of Judaism.

Jews believe God made a **covenant** with the ancient Israelites, or Hebrews. They believe God has chosen them to be a "light" to other nations, meaning a good example for others to follow.

The three traditional, or main, branches of Judaism are:

✡ Orthodox Jews, who believe the **Torah** is God's word and must be adhered to fully

✡ Conservative Jews, who believe the Torah is God's word but that some of the laws can be adapted

✡ Reform Jews, who believe the Torah was inspired by God but written by man, so they can follow their conscience where the laws are concerned.

Orthodox Jews follow strict rules about clothing and how they wear their hair.

Religious Beliefs

Important beliefs for Jews are the belief in one god, God, and the belief in the importance of serving God.

God

Jews believe that God is the one true god. They believe that God:

✡ controls nature and history

✡ is eternal, which means he lives forever

✡ knows everything

✡ is everywhere

✡ has no physical form

✡ loves the Jewish people

✡ provided Scriptures and laws that Jews and non-Jews must obey

✡ sent **prophets** to Earth, such as Moses

✡ will send the **Messiah**.

Jews do not believe that **Jesus** is the Messiah. They believe the Messiah will be a **descendant** of King David and King Solomon. The Messiah will gather all the Jews from all over Earth, bring them to Israel, and rebuild the Temple in Jerusalem. The time of the Messiah will be a time of world peace, without suffering and disease.

Jews have many different names for God. These include:
Elohim
El Elyon
Jehovah
Adonai
El Shaddai
El Roi

The Temple in Jerusalem was destroyed by the Romans in about 70 CE.

Religious Roles

Two of the ways that a Jew can serve the community in religious life are as a rabbi or as a cantor.

Rabbis

The word "rabbi" means "my teacher" or "my master." Rabbis are usually men but there are some female rabbis in Conservative and Reform synagogues.

Rabbis go to **theological college** and choose the subjects they need for the type of rabbi they want to be. They may choose to be a pulpit rabbi, who conducts religious services and is head of the Jewish community. They may choose to be a shahet, which is rabbi who performs the ritual slaughter of animals. Training to be a rabbi takes from two to four years.

Rabbis conduct religious services, teach, and counsel members of the Jewish community. They may also conduct special ceremonies, such as baby namings, **Bar Mitzvahs**, weddings, and funerals.

Cantors

Cantors are people who sing prayers solo and lead the **congregation** in singing. Cantors are always men in Orthodox synagogues but can be men or women in Reform or Conservative synagogues.

Cantors have voice lessons to learn to breathe and sing properly. Opera singers sometimes learn breathing and singing techniques from Jewish cantors.

This rabbi leads religious services.

A cantor leads the congregation in song and prayer.

7

Beliefs About Behavior

God gave Moses the Ten Commandments on two stone tablets.

Jews believe it is important to obey the Torah, particularly the Ten Commandments and the advice to give regularly to charity.

The Ten Commandments

God gave the Ten Commandments to Moses as a gift to the Jewish people. This was so they would know how to live a good and meaningful life.

Jews are also expected to study the scriptures, attend synagogue services, pray regularly, and say blessings after a meal. They must not harm one another, seek revenge, or judge people unfairly. Jews must pass on their beliefs to their children.

The Ten Commandments

1 Do not worship any other gods
2 Do not make any idols
3 Do not misuse the name of God
4 Keep the Sabbath holy
5 Honor your father and mother
6 Do not murder
7 Do not commit adultery
8 Do not kidnap
9 Do not lie
10 Do not be envious of another's belongings.

EXODUS 20:1–14

A plate is passed around
the congregation to collect
donations for a bride.

Giving to Charity

There is special advice in the Torah, the **Talmud** and the **Jewish Code of Law** about how Jews should give to charity:

✡ the money must be given to a person to help them become independent, such as giving them work

✡ it must be done in a way so that the person who receives the money does not lose self-respect

✡ it must be fair and just

✡ it is best if the person who receives the help does not know who donated the money

✡ the giver must not expect anything in return

✡ the minimum for giving to charity is one-tenth of one's earnings. So, for every fifty dollars earned, five dollars must go to charity.

Jews must also perform loving acts of kindness. These include inviting strangers to their home for meals and visiting sick people at home or in hospital. Jews also give financial help to brides who do not have parents or whose parents are very poor.

Scriptures

Jews believe the Hebrew scriptures, or the *Tanach*, are a gift from God to give them instruction in life. There are also books written to help interpret the Tanach.

The Tanach

"Tanach" is a made-up word, taken from the first letter of the three parts of the Hebrew Scriptures. The Tanach consists of:

✡ five books of the Torah (the Laws)

✡ eight books of the Nvi'im (the Prophets)

✡ eleven books of the K'tuvim (the Writings).

The Torah

The five books of the Torah were given to Moses on Mount Sinai and are known as the "laws of the Jews." The Torah is kept in a special cabinet called the Ark, which is the focus of the synagogue. A portion of the Torah is read each morning and afternoon of the Sabbath, and on Monday and Thursday mornings.

The Nvi'im

The Nvi'im is the longest section of the Tanach. It is a combination of historical events, religious teachings, and prophecies of the future.

The K'tuvim

The K'tuvim is also called the "Wisdom literature." It consists of poetry, history and discussions about why bad things happen to people, faith, reward, and punishment. Writers of the K'tuvim include King David, author of the Psalms, and King Solomon, who wrote the Proverbs.

When the Torah is taken out of the Ark it is carried around the synagogue.

A Jewish man studies the scriptures.

Interpreting the Tanach

A number of books have been written to help people interpret the Tanach. The three most important are the Midrash, the Mishnah, and the Talmud. They were originally passed down **orally** from teacher to student.

The Midrash

The Midrash interprets the Tanach by explaining the feelings and motives behind the writings. It includes stories to help explain important messages and tells some history that was not included in the Tanach. It was written down about 2,000 years ago.

The Mishnah

The Mishnah is a book of six sections discussing the Torah. It is written in the form of conversations about different issues, with each ending with a ruling. The Mishnah was written down after 70 CE. Its main author was Rabbi Juddah the Prince.

The Talmud

The Talmud includes the writings of rabbis from 200 to 500 CE. The rabbis studied the Tanach and wrote down their ideas about its message.

Religious Leaders

Two important Jewish religious leaders were Abraham and Moses.

Abraham 3819–3644 BCE

Abraham was the founding father of the Jewish nation. He was born in the city of Ur in Babylonia. He did not believe in worshipping many different gods as did his friends and family. In fact, Abraham smashed most of his father's **idols** to show him that they had no life or power.

Abraham only worshipped God, whom he believed was the one true god. God promised Abraham that if he left his home and family he would have many descendants who would become a whole new nation. Abraham did this and the covenant between God and the Jewish people began.

Abraham had two sons, Isaac and Ishmael. Isaac was born to Abraham's wife, Sarah. Jews believe Isaac is the **ancestor** of the Jewish people. Ishmael was the son of Abraham and his wife's maidservant, Hagar. Muslims believe Ishmael is the ancestor of the Arab people.

This is an early picture of Abraham and his two sons, Isaac and Ishmael.

God passed down the Ten Commandments to Moses on Mount Sinai.

Moses   1393–1272 BCE

Moses was born in the 1300s BCE in Egypt. His parents were Israelites who were **persecuted** by the Egyptians. When the Pharaoh ordered that all newborn Israelite boys be killed, Moses's mother placed Moses in a watertight basket on the river Nile. He was rescued by the Pharaoh's daughter, who took Moses to live in the royal palace.

Moses is best remembered for persuading the Pharaoh to let the Israelites leave Egypt. Moses followed God's directions to perform miracles that persuaded the Pharaoh. These miracles included turning the Nile into a river of blood and sending plagues of frogs and locusts to Egypt.

Moses led the Israelites out of Egypt, and performed more miracles, including:

✡ parting the Red Sea so the Israelites could cross it

✡ asking for, and receiving from God, food for the Israelites to eat while in the desert. The Israelites called this food "manna from Heaven."

God explained to Moses how he wanted the Israelites to behave. God gave Moses the Ten Commandments and the Torah, whose teachings Jews still follow today.

Worship Practices

Two important worship practices for Jews are observing the Sabbath and attending synagogue.

The Sabbath

The Scriptures teach that God created the world in six days and rested on the seventh. God told the Jews that the seventh day of the week must be a day of rest. They call this day the Sabbath, or Shabbat. For Jews, the Sabbath begins at sunset on Friday and ends at sunset on Saturday.

On the Friday night, Shabbat candles are lit, a special meal is served, and blessings are said. The family drinks wine and eats challah, which is a braided loaf of bread. Saturday is spent praying, studying, and spending time with family and friends. The day ends with a special ritual at nightfall, called the Havdalah. This includes drinking a glass of wine, saying a prayer of blessing, and lighting a special braided candle, called a Havdalah candle.

Challah, candles, and wine are placed on the table every Friday night.

HAVDALAH BLESSING

Blessed are you, Oh Lord our God, King of the Universe, who distinguishes between the sacred and the mundane, between light and dark, between Israel and the nations, between the seventh day and the six days of labor.
Blessed are You, Lord, who distinguishes between the sacred and the mundane.

Worshipping at a Synagogue

On the Sabbath, Jews go to the synagogue. The service is led by a rabbi and a cantor and is held in Hebrew or a mix of Hebrew and English. At an Orthodox synagogue, men and women sit separately and the scriptures are read aloud by men. In Conservative and Reform synagogues, women can also read the scriptures aloud and men and women can sit together.

The *Amidah*

One of the main Jewish prayers is the *Amidah*. This is a series of blessings for things such as good health, spirituality, and thanking God for his blessings. Jews stand and face Jerusalem when they recite the *Amidah*.

Torah Portions

Each week, a portion of the Torah is read so that the entire Torah scroll is read over one year. In synagogues all over the world, the same portion is read and studied. The scroll is wound back to the beginning after the High Holy days in September and October. A set reading from the Nvi'im, known as the HafTorah, accompanies the Torah portion.

The Torah scroll

This is a typical floor plan of an Orthodox Jewish synagogue.

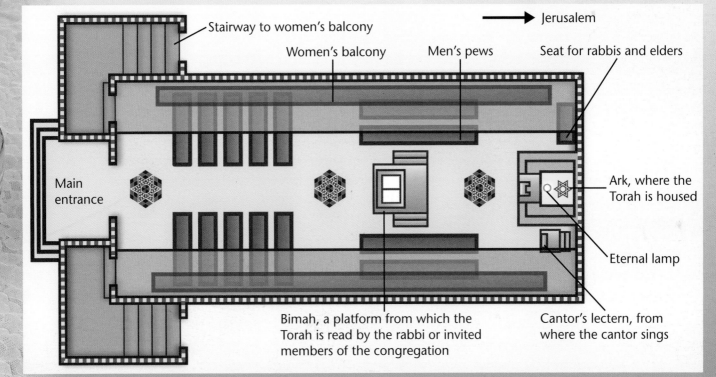

Stairway to women's balcony

→ Jerusalem

Women's balcony

Men's pews

Seat for rabbis and elders

Main entrance

Ark, where the Torah is housed

Eternal lamp

Bimah, a platform from which the Torah is read by the rabbi or invited members of the congregation

Cantor's lectern, from where the cantor sings

Yom Kippur is an important holy day in the Jewish calendar.

Festivals and Celebrations

Two important times of the year for Jews are the High Holy Days and Hanukkah.

The High Holy Days

Rosh Hashanah, or the Jewish New Year, is the first of the High Holy Days. It begins ten days of self-examination, when each individual thinks over the mistakes they have made over the past Jewish year. These can be wrong actions they chose to do, or helpful actions that they did not do. During the High Holy Days, Jews have to atone for, or put right, whatever they did wrong. The last day of the High Holy Days is Yom Kippur, or the Day of Atonement. This is when Jews say sorry to God.

Jews eat a large and festive meal on the eve of Yom Kippur. They then **fast** from sunset to sunset, but only if they are healthy. No one is allowed to risk their health by not eating or drinking.

The Talmud mentions additional restrictions that Jews should observe during Yom Kippur. These include:

✡ not wearing leather shoes

✡ not washing or bathing

✡ not putting oils, such as perfumes, on their bodies.

After Yom Kippur, Jews feel calm and believe they are more connected with their true selves.

The tallest candle on the menorah, called the Shamash, is used to light another candle each night over the eight nights of Hanukkah.

Many Jewish children enjoy playing with a dreidel.

Hanukkah

Hanukkah is an eight-day celebration which happens in November or December. It commemorates a time in about 200 BCE, when the Temple in Jerusalem had just been liberated after a battle. According to the Talmud, there was only enough holy oil to light the **menorah** in the Temple for one day. Miraculously, the menorah was still burning eight days later, which was the length of time it took to prepare more holy oil.

Jews celebrate Hanukkah by lighting a candle on the menorah each night for eight nights. Special prayers are also said to thank God.

During Hanukkah, children play with a spinning top, called a dreidel. Food cooked in oil is eaten during this time. Popular foods include jam doughnuts and potato pancakes, called latkes.

The Jewish or Hebrew calendar is different from the Western **Gregorian calendar**. Therefore, Jewish holy days fall on different dates in the Gregorian calendar each year. Here are some of the major Jewish celebrations:

Purim (Festival of Lots)
Adar 14
February or March

Passover
Seven- or eight-day festival
Nisan 15 to 23
March or April

Rosh Hashanah (Jewish New Year)
Tishrei 1
September

Aseret Yemei Teshuva (Ten Days of Repentance)
For ten days between Rosh Hashanah and Yom Kippur
September or October

Yom Kippur (Day of Atonement)
Tishrei 10
September or October

Hanukkah (Festival of Lights)
Kislev 25 to Tevet 2 or 3
November or December

Important Jews

Two important Jews who are remembered for their work are Rabbi Dr Abraham Geiger and Anne Frank.

Rabbi Dr. Abraham Geiger 1810–1874

Dr. Geiger was a German rabbi who was one of the founding leaders for Reform Judaism. He lived at a time when many young Jews were abandoning their faith because they found the laws and rituals too difficult to follow. Dr. Geiger looked for ways to make the Jewish faith more modern and attractive to them.

Dr. Geiger taught that Jews did not have to avoid non-Jews and that morals are more important than rituals. He encouraged Jews to play musical instruments in the synagogue on the Sabbath and encouraged them to pray in their own language instead of only in Hebrew. Dr. Geiger taught that the **sermon** is the most important part of a religious service.

Dr. Geiger encouraged Jews to think of Judaism as a growing, changing religion that could co-exist in modern society.

Dr. Geiger was important to the modernization of Judaism.

Anne Frank   1929–1945

Annelies Marie "Anne" Frank was a German-born Reform Jewish girl. Anne and her family were forced into hiding during the German occupation of Holland in World War II. Anne, her family, and four others spent 25 months in an annex of rooms above her father's office in Amsterdam. They were eventually betrayed to the **Nazis**, arrested, and deported to **concentration camps**. Anne's father was the only survivor of the group and Anne died of typhus at Bergen-Belsen.

Anne Frank kept a diary which recorded her day-to-day life during this terrifying time. She described the difficulties of living when Jews were forced to wear yellow stars and hand in their bicycles. They were not allowed to catch trams, go to the theater, or visit the homes of Christians for fear of arrest. Anne described the difficulties of growing up when confined to small quarters, where she had to be quiet all day, did not have enough to eat, and knew that one false move could lead to their arrest and the arrest of the people who were helping them.

Anne's diary was saved by one of the family's helpers and was first published in 1947. Today her diary is one of the most widely read books in the world, is the most popular war documentary of World War II, and has been translated into 67 languages.

Anne Frank's diary gave millions of readers an insight into life as a Jewish girl hiding out during World War II.

Clothes and Food

The choice of clothes worn to the synagogue is an important tradition to Jews. Jewish men and women are encouraged to dress modestly at all times, especially when visiting the synagogue. There are also rules that many Jews follow about which foods are **kosher**.

Clothes for Jewish Men

Some Jewish men wear a yarmulke, or skullcap, at all times, while others may only wear one at a synagogue. Orthodox men may also wear a shtreimel. This is a black fur hat worn to the synagogue on the Sabbath. At the synagogue, Orthodox men also wear a tallith and tefillin. A tallith is a prayer shawl worn over the shoulders, with special knotted fringes hanging from the corners. The fringes are called tzitzit, and represent the laws of the Torah. The tefillin are two small leather boxes that contain passages from the Torah. The boxes are attached to the head and arm by leather straps.

The tefillin can be seen on the foreheads of these Jewish men.

Clothes for Jewish Women

Orthodox married women almost always cover their heads with a scarf or a wig. Orthodox Jews consider it very forward for a woman to show her hair to anyone but her husband. Women in Reform or Conservative synagogues may also wear a tallith and a yarmulke but do not cover their hair.

Women wear scarves over their heads when praying at the Wailing Wall.

Food

Many Jews follow rules regarding which food is kosher, or fit to eat. These rules come from the Torah and from later writings by rabbis. Some of the kosher rules are:

✡ Jews must only eat animals with **cloven hooves** that chew their cud, such as cows, sheep, and deer. This means Jews cannot eat animals such as pigs, camels, or rabbits

✡ animals must be killed ritually, in a humane way

✡ Jews must not eat animals that are diseased, which kosher butchers check for carefully

✡ Jews must not serve or eat meals that include both dairy products and meat, such as a cheese and beef hamburger. There must be a separate set of dishes for meat and a separate set of dishes for milk products.

Ritual Slaughter of Animals

A shohet is a rabbi trained in the ritual slaughter of animals for food. Before killing the animal, the shohet checks it carefully for diseases. He then cuts the animal's jugular vein using a special knife so that it faints and dies quickly. The shohet then makes sure that as much blood drains out of the animal as possible. This is because it is not kosher for Jews to eat blood.

Food plays an important role in the ritual of the Passover Seder meal.

Birth

Important ceremonies for Jewish children include the Bris milah, the naming and **circumcision** ceremony for boys, and the Brit ha Bat, a naming ceremony for girls.

Bris Milah

The Bris milah ceremony is usually performed eight days after a boy is born, unless he is unwell.

The godparent, called the sandek, holds the baby boy. A specially trained **mohel** blesses the baby and quickly performs the circumcision. Traditionally, the boy is given gauze soaked in wine to suck on to ease the pain. Less traditional mohels use a mild anaesthetic cream.

After the circumcision, the boy is named and blessed and a special celebratory meal is served, called the seudat mitzvah.

Members of the congregation place their hands on the baby to bless him after the ceremonial circumcision.

Brit ha Bat

Reform Jews have a naming ceremony for girls, called the
Brit ha Bat, which can be performed at home or at the synagogue.
Brit ha Bat is performed eight to thirty days after the birth,
depending on how long the mother needs to recover. A rabbi
usually presides over the ceremony.

The Brit ha Bat ceremony includes:

✡ the reciting of the psalms

✡ a blessing for the girl

✡ dancing and singing in honor of the new baby.

Girls will usually be given a Hebrew name.

Orthodox families name their daughter when they are called up
for the reading of the Torah in the synagogue. This happens on a
Sabbath or a weekday when the Torah is read.

Growing Up

Two important celebrations for young people growing up are the bar mitzvah for boys, and the **bat mitzvah** for girls. They become responsible for their own actions and their observances of the Torah.

Bar Mitzvah

Bar mitzvah is the celebration for a boy growing up. The ceremony takes place when a boy is about thirteen years old. This is when he is allowed to read aloud from the Torah in Hebrew at the synagogue. Being called up to read aloud from the Torah is considered an honor. A groom on the eve of his wedding or a person on his or her birthday may be asked to read from the Torah.

A boy prepares for his bar mitzvah by attending classes to study Hebrew and Jewish history and law. After his bar mitzvah, the Jewish community considers him a man.

On the day of his bar mitzvah, the boy will wear a tefillin and a tallith. The ceremony usually ends with a party, presents, dancing, and speeches from family members and friends.

A Jewish boy holds the Torah at his bar mitzvah.

Bat Mitzvah

In the Reform and Conservative synagogues, the bat mitzvah is almost identical to the bar mitzvah. When a girl is twelve or thirteen years old she can read aloud from the Torah in Hebrew in the synagogue. Like boys, she must prepare for this day by attending classes to study the Hebrew language and Jewish history and law. The girl wears a tallith around her shoulders while she reads. This ceremony usually ends with a party, presents, dancing, and speeches from family members and friends.

Orthodox Jewish girls celebrate their bat mitzvahs with a party. There is no public reading of the Torah.

Bar and bat mitzvahs are not just held for teenagers. **Converts** and Jews who chose not to have this ceremony in their youth can also have the ceremony when they are older.

A pointer, or yad, is used to hold one's place when reading from the Torah, as the sacred scroll should not be touched directly.

Marriage

There are many traditions that are practiced at Jewish weddings.

Beliefs About Marriage

Jews see marriage as a holy and legal union. Men and women have the right to choose their own partners. Even when a matchmaker is used, a woman can refuse a groom who has been chosen for her. Jews also believe that the rabbi does not marry the bride and groom, but that they marry each other with the rabbi's help.

Divorce has always been permitted in Judaism. The Torah provides a procedure for divorce if the marriage is not fulfilling.

Wedding Clothes

A Jewish bride wears a white dress to symbolize purity and a headdress and veil, although this varies depending on the country in which she lives. Orthodox brides must wear a dress that covers their shoulders.

Jewish grooms usually wear a black suit and a yarmulke. Male guests at the wedding are also expected to wear a yarmulke. At an Orthodox wedding, the groom wears a kittel, which is a short white linen robe, over his suit.

Wedding Ceremony

Jewish couples are married under a chuppah, or canopy. The chuppah symbolizes the home that they will build together.

The couple is led to the chuppah by their parents. The bride circles the groom seven times. This is to symbolize that the bride will become a protective light surrounding her new household.

The rabbi recites blessings over a cup of wine. The couple drinks the wine and the groom puts a ring on the bride's finger. The rabbi reads the marriage contract and the couple shares a second cup of wine to symbolize that they will share a life together. The rabbi gives the couple advice on married life.

The groom then breaks a glass under his foot to symbolize the destruction of the Temple in Jerusalem. This is because even though this is a happy occasion, Jews must always remember the destruction of Jerusalem. Once the glass is broken, the congregation shouts "Mazel tov!," which means "Congratulations!"

After the wedding, there is a party with music, dancing, and usually, a four-course meal.

The groom breaks a glass wrapped in a linen napkin under his foot at a Jewish wedding ceremony.

Death and the Afterlife

Judaism has many traditions after someone has died. Jews also believe there is a life after death.

The Funeral

Jewish funerals are organized as soon as possible after a person has died. The body is cleaned, dressed in plain white linen, and placed in a simple coffin. Jewelry is removed and given to the family. The ceremony consists of a prayer to praise God, psalms recited from the Bible, and a speech praising the deceased. Traditionally, Jews place the head of the deceased so the person is buried facing Israel. Orthodox and Conservative Jews do not allow cremation.

After the funeral, there is a seven-day mourning period, called shivah. Friends and family visit the home of the deceased and sit on low chairs. The family does not attend any parties for thirty days, to show respect to the deceased. During the mourning period, mourners lead certain prayers at the synagogue.

For a person whose parent has died, mourning lasts for twelve months. They must recite the **Kaddish** at the synagogue regularly during this time.

Every year, on the anniversary of the person's death, a special candle is lit. The candle burns for twenty-four hours and a shorter version of the Kaddish, called the memorial Kaddish, is recited by the family.

Traditionally, six to eight pallbearers carry the coffin from the funeral service to the grave.

Jews believe they must do good for its own sake, such as donating money in charity boxes.

Life After Death

Jews believe in an afterlife, but descriptions of the afterlife are not mentioned in detail in the Hebrew Scriptures. Most Jews believe it is important to obey God in this life and that the afterlife should not be the focus. They must do good for its own sake. Good should not be done merely as an incentive to go to heaven.

Jews do believe that people have an eternal soul. If they have followed God's commandments they will be rewarded by going to a wonderful place called the Garden of Eden.

The Garden of Eden

The Garden of Eden is also called heaven. It is a place where one feels the peace of having followed the rules of Jewish laws and lived a good life. Jews believe that when souls reach the Garden of Eden they will experience God's presence and be very happy.

Judaism Around the World

Today, there are approximately 14 million Jews worldwide. Jews can be found in many countries including the United States, Israel, Europe, South America, South Africa, Australia, Turkey, and Britain.

Most Jews live in the United States and Israel. Forty percent of the Jews in the world live in the United States. Forty-one percent of Jews live in Israel.

This map shows the top ten countries where Jews live throughout the world.

ARCTIC OCEAN

ARCTIC OCEAN

UNITED KINGDOM
2 percent

RUSSIAN FEDERATION
2 percent

CANADA
3 percent

UNITED STATES OF AMERICA
40 percent

FRANCE
4 percent

GERMANY
1 percent

ISRAEL
41 percent

ATLANTIC OCEAN

PACIFIC OCEAN

PACIFIC OCEAN

BRAZIL
Less than 1 percent

AUSTRALIA
Less than 1 percent

INDIAN OCEAN

ARGENTINA
1 percent

N
W + E
S

KEY

▬	area of country
ISRAEL	name of country
41 percent	percentage of world's total Jewish population

SOUTHERN OCEAN

SOUTHERN OCEAN

Glossary

ancestor	a member of a family who lived a long time ago
bar mitzvah	a ceremony celebrating a boy's coming of age
bat mitzvah	a ceremony celebrating a girl's coming of age
circumcision	where the foreskin is removed from the penis
cloven hooves	divided feet on an animal
concentration camps	Nazi-run camps where Jews were forced to stay during World War II, where they were very badly treated and often killed
congregation	a group of people meeting to worship God
converts	people who change their religion
covenant	a sacred pact
cremation	the burning of a dead body until only ashes are left
descendant	offspring who descended from a person
fast	to not eat, or eat very little
Gregorian calendar	the most widely used calendar in the world, based on the cycle of the Sun
idols	images used as objects of worship
Jesus	a prophet whom Christians believe is the Messiah, but Jews do not
Jewish Code of Law	how Jews should conduct their everyday affairs
Kaddish	a prayer praising God and yearning for the establishment of God's Kingdom on Earth
kosher	permitted or lawful
menorah	a candlestick that holds seven or nine candles
Messiah	in Judaism, the savior of the Jews
mohel	a rabbi who performs circumcisions
Nazis	members of the National Socialist German Workers' Party, which was founded in Germany in 1919
orally	spoken rather than written
persecuted	treated badly because of one's religious beliefs
prophets	people through whom the will of God is expressed
scriptures	sacred books
sermon	a speech which teaches about a section of the Torah or other Scriptures
synagogues	Jewish places of worship
Talmud	a Jewish scripture
theological college	a college where you study God and religion
Torah	the first five books of the Jewish religious scriptures

Index